EXCEL PIVOT TABLES

Tips and Tricks to learn and Execute Excel PivotTables forBeginners

William Collins

Table of Contents

Introduction

First, I want to take a moment to say welcome to learning about PivotTables and to thank you for purchasing, along with taking the time to read this. I know that there are a lot of other Pivot Excel books out there and you chose this one. I promise you won't be disappointed.

Jumping right into the heart of what you bought this book for, let's talk about PivotTables. PivotTables can deal with large amounts of data and break it down into portion that are easier to understand. The PivotTable are unique from the regular data tables that you are used to because it allows you to pick and choose certain data aspects and for you to see it in different ways. A lot of people refer to it as "Slice and Dice".

PivotTables are also extremely user friendly in the fact that all you need to do is drag and drop. You don't need to make any command buttons or VBA Macros. You can even use the functions that are already programmed into the ribbon without having to do anything fancy.

In this book we will go into detail about how PivotTables work and how to use them in different ways. Included in this book we will show you how to create random data. This is for all those readers out there that can never seem to find the exact data that they want. Now, it is possible to create the data using a formula, rather than having to take the exorbitant amount of time that it would take you to create the fictitious data and it lowers the risk of there being a pattern without you realizing.

Also, I want to tell you that when ever we cover something or before we go onto a new portion of learning, I would like for you to take some time and explore what we have been working on, there are many that are available. This does sound weird but, the reasoning for this is so that you can go and work with some of the options that come with the teachings that are covered. This process, will allow you to familiarize yourself with what the program can do, allow you to become more confident in implementing what you want the program to do and will help you in personalizing your tables and graphs later on.

Before moving on to the rest of this book I would like to take the time to say thank you again with my deepest gratitude for purchasing this book. I truly do believe in sharing the knowledge that you have with anyone you can, because you never know what can influence someone to do better than they did the day before.

Chapter 1

How did PivotTables start?

Origins

To begin with, why don't we discuss how the idea of PivotTables came to be?

The answer to this question is that when program designer Pito Salas was one day looking over a datasheet while on the job, programming what would later become Lotus Improv, he noticed that there were patterns on that spreadsheet and he thought that there should be a way to bring them out, so that the data within the spreadsheet could be analyzed quickly. It was also so someone wouldn't have to go through the whole spreadsheet and pull out various pieces of data one at a time. The program was so that you could easily pick sections of data from your spread sheet and place them on a table to make it easier to create graphs, charts and dashboards.

Pito Salas was dubbed later on as the "Father of PivotTables" by Bill Jelen and Mike Alexander, authors of *PivotTable Data Crunching*.

When this all started back in 1991, Lotus Development started selling its NeXT program, which was followed soon after by Brio

Technology who developed and released the program called DataPivot for the Macintosh computer series, which was a couple of months after the NeXT release. Bio Technology, was actually the company able to get their technology patented in 1999. This was followed by the company, Borland, purchasing said technology afterwards and developing their own program Quattro Pro.

After all this happened, in 1993, Microsoft developed their own version of Improv and then in early 1994 when Microsoft updated and added the coding to Microsoft Excel 5, the original release of modern-day PivotTables. Afterward, Microsoft added different features that allowed you to do even more with the PivotTables. Later on, in the 1997 version of Excel included PivotTable Wizard that allowed you to add Macros to your PivotTables, along with the new ability to pivot cache objects and to calculate fields. Then the 2000's hit and you were able to move all that data on the PivotTables onto pivot charts. Making it even easier to design graphs, charts and even dashboards for your data.

Summary of What we will be covering

As a quick heads up on what we are going to be covering, incase you have some information that you happen to already have prepared for placing into tables, graphs and finally creating a dashboard; which is what we are truly aiming to create by the end of this book. Except, that isn't the only thing that this book is aiming to walk you though, this book is meant to enlighten you about the process of creating PivotTables, enabling PivotTables to display the information in a way that comes across easier and what the PivotTables can do for you instead of you having to go through process, after long process, of making different charts and then adding them onto a page that isn't interactive.

What PivotTable allows you to do

Like it was stated previously, PivotTable allows you to extrapolate data quickly and efficiently, because all the data is already in the correct spots. So, there is no need for VBA coding or downloading extra add ons. Simple, huh?

Terms That You Should Know

Chart	Chart refers to any of the graphs that we reference or create within this book.
Dashboard	A page within an Excel workbook that displays data from within the Workbook.
Data	Refers to any of the information that is contained within the workbook, or what we have the computer reference to.
Fields	When making a PivotTable, Fields are the equivalent to the headers of the data you are using.

Function	Equations they you type into a cell on a spreadsheet that allows you to preform a task that is already programmed into the Excel program.
Quadrant	When you get to the PivotTable Fields menu, there are 4 different areas (Filter, Columns, Rows and Values) that you can place your fields into.
Slicer	An interactive button that allows you to pick and choose the data that you are looking at on a Dashboard. They allow you to "slice and dice" data.
Spread Sheet	Where all your data, charts and PivotTables will be located.
Table	Sets of data that will, not change and you can use as a reference in an equation.
Workbook	This is where all your data, dashboard, PivotTables and charts will be located.

Just as a side note there will be more vocabulary terms later on but as to not overwhelm you, we are going to slowly dip you into the waters.

Starting Up

For most of this book we are going to use the scenario that you own a pet supply company with chains. However, we are going to start off small scale and only going to start off on the small scale of one store in particular, before we move on to a larger set of data that will allow us to go onto creating an interactive dashboard.

But, to give an example of one of the things that we are going to be able to do is take our data and see what our cashiers' average sale is. We could also see what the favorite pet for that particular store is, or even which cashier has the highest sales.

Fields of View

This little subtitle sounds a bit weird, but it ties in I promise. When you have your data with all it's headers, those headers turn into what the computer later on calls fields. Promise it will make more sense later on.

So, when making a PivotTable, when you click on the insert button, there are two different methods that you can choose from, the first option allows you to choose one of the tables offered by Excel; or you can choose to make one on your own. Though before making a PivotTable there is a bit of information that we have to cover and explain before taking that step.

Let's say that you chose to make your own PivotTable from scratch, Excel will have a window pop, asking what the area is that you want the computer to pull the data from and it will give you two more options as to choose to make your PivotTable being placed on the spread sheet that you are already occupying or to place the table on a brand-new sheet. You can do either but, throughout this book what is going to be happening is that all the PivotTables will be placed on a new sheet. Truthfully, it's easier to flip back and forth between the tabs, than the pain of having all your PivotTables on one sheet and trying to scroll back and forth on that one sheet.

Adding on to this is the fact that you are going to see a new mini window in the right side of the window of Excel, the image shown is what appears; it shows all your columns in a scrolling list box. Those columns in your data table have now turned into "Field" options for you to drag and drop to the area below. That area is a little interactive chart that will remind you of when you were back in math class and will remind you of quadrants in Algebra class.

As you can see from the picture there are four different areas at the bottom of the window labeled Filters, Columns, Rows and ∑Values. You can select any of your fields from your list above and place them into the chart area. See, simple drag and drop.

With the first example that I am going to create and show, I had to create an assortment of random data. Don't worry, I will show you how to create your own random data as well, so if you need to later, you can make your own random data too. Within that random data were the categories of: Cashier, Pet (type), Sale and number of items.

Originally for this demo I selected *Cashiers* to go into the rows and *Sales* went into the values field. What came out is a nice table, showing the cashiers sales for those transactions. But I took it one step further and placed the data *Number of Items* into the columns area. What comes out is an amazing table that you can alter at in an instant.

Sum of Sale	Column Labels											
Row Labels	Ball Python	Bearded Dragon	Budgie/Parakeet	Cat	Dog	Ferret	Fish	Hamster	Parrot	Saltwater	Grand Total
Carol	78.9			87.16	192.5	115.6	37.12	64.92	101.5	160.58	64.45	902.73
Chloe	236.7	21.5		130.74	96.25	173.4	37.12	64.92		245.87	126.9	1130.4
David	236.7	10.75		43.58		115.6	111.36	21.64	304.5	160.58	126.9	1133.61
Georgiana	315.6	21.5				173.4	17.12	21.64	101.5	160.58	128.9	960.34
Lacey		43		37.16	365	57.8	74.24	21.64	406	321.16		1396
Lisa	78.9	21.5			288.75	57.8	37.12				128.9	612.97
Merlin	157.8				288.75		37.12	43.28	101.5	80.29	64.45	771.19
Mike	236.7	21.5		43.58		115.4		21.64	101.5	160.58		701.1
Shawn	315.6	21.5		130.74	192.5			21.64	101.5	80.29		863.77
Tyler	236.7	10.75				173.4	74.24		101.5		64.45	661.04
Grand Total	1893.6	172		522.96	1443.75	982.6	445.44	281.32	1319.5	1364.91	708.95	9135.05

9

You can also change the sales from being plain numbers to numbers with the dollar sign and even change it to percentage and so on. All that extra stuff will be shown later on in detail. Take a look at the pictures added to see some of the steps that was just described.

I included a way to show you a method of creating random data and some websites that offer to create some the random data for you, those websites will be listed at the end of the book. The reason that the method of creating random data is being offered, is because most of the time, when you search for random data bases to practice with there aren't many or it could have too little or too much data. Though this is due to the fact that most companies won't share their reports on inventory, sales or client records due to business policies.

We are still going to need an extra-large amount of data in order to create the dashboard later on, the first set of data is just going to have about one hundred and fifty lines of data.

A bit of History

Before jumping into creating our random data, do you happen to know when the first graph was created? The answer to this question may surprise you.

First, let's introduce the inventor of the graph. The man's name was William Playfair and, in his lifetime, amazingly he didn't just create graphs. William Playfair was a Scottish engineer that had assisted Great Britain during its war with France. For a little bit of background England and France have been fighting on and off since the 1100's, the time period that William Playfair assisted in was the French Revolution (1789-1799).

What did William Playfair do you ask? He was a SPY and he assisted in the circulation of counterfeit French currency (Iivier), causing the whole French economy to collapse in 1793. The currency of the modern Franc (now substituted for the Euro in 2002), did not come out until a little later in 1803, though there were several versions in between.

So, did William Playfair create the first graph? The answer: 1786.

William designed the first Line, Area and Bar charts for Economic Data. After that William Playfair also created the pie charts and circle graphs in 1801, they were to show parts of a whole. If you did not take notice the years mentioned, between publishing these charts he was being a spy and colapsing the French currency.

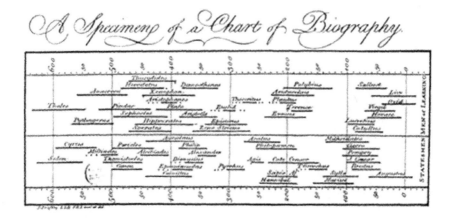

Coincidentally before this, there was only timelines, created about twenty years beforehand which didn't look like the modern timelines we have today, they looked like odd versions of a family tree. The timeline chart of yesteryear did not have only one line to place extra tangents off of it, but an area that was measured out and allowed you to place lines for the length of a person's life or the length of the war. Sort of like how Greek mythology said the Fates measured your life by a length of string. Note: the picture featured here was borrowed from one of the Microsoft web pages.

Chapter 2

Randomizing Data

Creating the Random

As it was just stated, you are going to learn how to create your own random data that, thankfully, you don't have to enter in cell by cell. By just using Excel's ability to use a cell with a function and then have it repeat that function over and over allows us the ability do this. Though it is a bit of a process at first, it is worth it in the fact that you do not have to come up with a large portion of the data. You do not need to worry about having too many parts of that data repeating itself, which is what happens more often than not in human created data.

To start off with we are going to set up a table, but not just some random table, you are going to want the first two columns to be titled, in bold, with the headers Value and Range. Then we are going to keep with the theme of Pet Supply Chain, place a heading for Cashiers, Sales, and what type of pet. We are going to use these for a simple PivotTable.

Value	Range	Cashier	Sales	Type of Pet

Value	Range
0	0-.1
.1	.1-.2
.2	.2-.3
.3	.3-.4
.4	.4-.5
.5	.5-.6
.6	.6-.7
.7	.7-.8
.8	.8-.9
.9	.9-1
1	None

Under the Value header you are going to enter the information going at 0.1 increments 0 to 1. Next under the Range header in the first cell below it place 0-0.1 hit enter and keep going up in increments until you have that column filled down to where you have the .9 in the previous column. In the cell next to 1 place the word none in it. With this set up it allows us to use a function that references a portion of the table we are creating. The decimal that we will randomly create later will fall within the ranges of this section of the table that we just started.

For the next four columns you are going to pick 10 names, 10 different sale totals, and 10 different types of pets. I'm not going to have you copy the names and numbers that I used because no matter what it won't be the same as mine. This is do the function that we are going to use to create the decimal numbers to correspond to the table.

The =RAND() function that you can use through Excel allows you to evenly distribute random numbers between 0-1, the numbers are decimals are four to five positions form the decimal (example: .26589). If you think about it, this method creates an infinite number of possibilities, and your data will never repeat until you have gone through thousands upon thousands of options.

Also with the =RAND() function the number will change every time that you enter new information, your page updates (this is a function that occurs in Excel without you having to do anything) or if you hit the F9 key (which has the function that allows you to calculate all the equations on the page). If you like you can learn more about this in the other book *Excel VBA*, the book will also teach you about the language that Excel uses, Visual Basics for Applications.

As you can see the that what was created is not fancy, pretty simple and is not yet a table. To turn it into a table we need to highlight from Value to the cell below ball python. When you do this there should be a little icon that looks like a file box at the bottom right of those now highlighted cells. The icon is called the quick analysis icon and if you click it, it gives you several different options but the one that we want is labeled tables. Under that label are two different options, one is to create a table and the other is to go directly to a PivotTable, but we don't have any actual data on this table so it would be useless to actually click on the PivotTable icon.

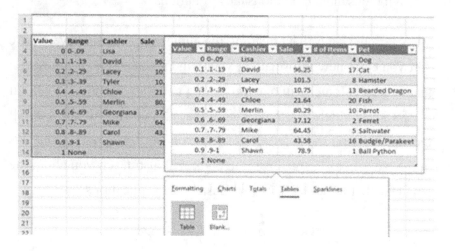

As you can see from the picture provided our table is displayed before we even create it.

Another way for you to create a table is to hit the Ctrl + t keys. This is an older way to create a table quick and easy, there are a number of other functions that you can do by using the control button, a couple will be listed throughout the book and a chart will be made towards the end of the book that will contain this and other keyboard combinations.

Value	Range	Cashier	Sale	Pet
0	0-.09	Lisa	46.95	Dog
0.1	.1-.19	Donald	53.8	Cat
0.2	.2-.29	Lacy	64.98	Lizard
0.3	.3-.39	Tyler	92.5	Bird
0.4	.4-.49	Chloe	76.81	Small Animal
0.5	.5-.59	Merlin	16.96	Invertibre
0.6	.6-.69	Georgiana	82.98	Freshwater Fish
0.7	.7-.79	Mike	31.97	Saltwater Fish
0.8	.8-.89	Carol	18.44	Snake
0.9	.9-1	Shawn	28.11	Exotic
1	None			

Feel free if you like to change up the features of the table, you can change its color or the font within it, even the type of barriers on the cells. Anything you want, it does not have to look like mine. The process of changing it up will allow you to familiarize yourself with the Excel program a bit more and make it more appealing for yourself.

Now comes the part that is going to allow you to randomly place all the information in our table. First create a new sheet, the reason for this is so you don't have to keep scrolling around on the same page as your table, we can name the sheet so we know which one we want at any given time and it allow you to see clearly what it is that we are doing. Next we are going to place labels in the first 3 columns with Random1, Random2 and Random3, you don't have to make them bold but it is suggested because Excel can differentiate between a header and regular data. The labels in the next three

17

columns follow with the headers that we placed on the table that we created earlier, Cashier, Sale, and Pet.

Now that we have set up for the randomizing of your data, select the first cell under Random 1 and enter the formula from before into your ribbon:

$$= Rand()$$

As it was explained earlier, the formula allows you to have the computer pick a random number between 0 and 1. Now, that you have gotten that first random number into the first cell, there is a little square in the bottom right of your cell, double click it and drag across until you reach the column Random3.

Random1	Random2	Random3
0.289003	0.493576	0.016803
0.364515	0.949465	0.575214
0.904809	0.601099	0.895541
0.426089	0.786577	0.278109
0.970172	0.391033	0.275692
0.030172	0.578074	0.79224
0.834707	0.148518	0.612407
0.359783	0.864718	0.680122
0.575225	0.040708	0.180552
0.177342	0.630623	0.900622
0.037478	0.17313	0.444624
0.072288	0.303035	0.562917
0.513072	0.815949	0.268873
0.012632	0.29587	0.643942
0.471232	0.771847	0.642433
0.008652	0.115353	0.507678
0.152774	0.220373	0.175495
0.25476	0.020152	0.464869
0.811913	0.676638	0.662981

If this was done correctly you should have a line of random decimals going across your first three columns, then doing the same process with the little box on the bottom right, still keeping all the cells previously highlighted as so, and drag the little square down 150 rows from where we are now. So, now that you now have 600 cells filled with 600 different numbers, it's time to fill them in with random data.

Start by selecting the cell below the column labeled Cashier and enter this code, though mind you, if you were playing around with the options earlier and changed the name of your table you'll need to switch it out with the table_1 part.

$$= VLookup(A3, Table1, 3, True)$$

I know that all this looks like a bunch of gibberish written in Greek or even VBA, but we are going to be breaking the formula down for you, so that you know what it is you are asking the computer to do.

= is to set up for the computer to place the answer for the equation into the cell that you have currently selected and are typing in. VLOOKUP is to tell the computer that it is to reference the next thing that we key in. The next part is in parenthesis, that means that whatever is inside it is where and how we want the computer to answer. Within the parenthesis we have A3, which is the location of the random number that we created earlier. Next we have the name of the table that we created Table_1 (or whatever you chose to name your table), it will also appear in the little drop-down menu as you start to type, it pops up whenever you start to type in a formula. The number three represents the third column on the table that we are

19

using, that column in your table should have all the Cashiers names listed. Lastly in the coding we have True, in this equation it means that the computer is going to approximate to the closest range on the table. See how we did that? With us placing a range on the table the computer can now use the table as a decoder with the random numbers that we set up and give us an answer.

	A	B	C	D	E	F	G	H
1								
2	Random1	Random2	Random3	Random4	Sales Person	Sales	# of Items	Pet
3	0.043379	0.043839	0.352543	0.417621	=VLOOKUP(A3,Table_1,3,TRUE)			
4	0.259119	0.96526	0.792225	0.763238				
5	0.927025	0.598838	0.832774	0.893975				
6	0.616661	0.423495	0.296267	0.050784				
7	0.249087	0.846245	0.335089	0.544352				
8	0.77754	0.995671	0.494193	0.149727				
9	0.652703	0.74985	0.187391	0.679116				

1Note: this picture is an extra so that I can show you how it will look on your screen. Do Not follow the formula in it.

In the picture that is featured, you can see that everything is as described and that A3 is highlighted in blue on the sheet and in the equation. The result of our equation going correctly, mind you your result will not be the exact same as mine, will have the name of one of cashiers that you listed in your table. If you don't get a name from the equation but get a little exclamation point in the top left and a word in all caps following a pound sign (or for those who now recognize it as a hashtag), this means that the equation was typed in incorrectly somewhere and needs to be re-entered. One example of this is #REF, it means that the reference that the equation was told to cite from, is either no longer available or that some of the data that you were using in the equation no longer exists.

Remember if you didn't do anything to your table aside from color and change it's appearance, there should be no reason that this formula will not work.

What we need to do now is to set the random data so that it doesn't change. With the equation being random every time that you enter new information into the spreadsheet or if you hit the F9 key (which is telling the Excel program to calculate all the equations in the worksheet), it updates itself and the number changes. Once the number changes the answer that we got before changes as well. We don't want, the data to change because that would mean that the charts that we are going to make would just keep changing and we don't want the dashboard to be interactive that way.

We are going to highlight all the cells that have the random numbers in them again, you are going to copy this set of numbers. In newer Excel programs it gives you the option of pasting just the values onto the spreadsheet (along with a few other options). However, in the older programs you might have to do something a little different.

After right clicking on your highlighted cells, on the little menu, there should be an option called paste special, right underneath the regular paste option. The reason that we want this is because if we just use the normal copy and paste it won't work, I could not find a reason as to why and tried to look up the reason for this, but it was not meant to be so. My best theory is that when you copy the random numbers, you are not actually copying the random numbers that you see but the equation that we assigned to those cells and the computer doesn't know how to copy and paste that.

Once you have clicked on the special paste option, a message box should appear and offer a couple of different options. You want the one that says values, so that it converts the formulas that we have placed into the spreadsheet to the values that are displayed, currently on your sheet. Did it work for you? Great if it did. If not try again. If you need to you can copy and paste to a new sheet if necessary.

Returning to the top of the cashier's column, left click twice on the little square in the bottom right of the selected cell and drag it all the way down to the bottom of our list, the whole column should be filled with the cashier's names now. Following the trend go back up to the top of the sheet where the headers are and double clicking again on the first cell under the cashier's column drag the little square on the bottom right over toward the pets column, this should copy the formula from the cashiers column and paste it in the sales column. With this method though it doesn't change the formula automatically to switch to the other columns in your table, it will copy the formula for the cashiers correctly from one cell to the next.

We fix this little hiccup by clicking on each of the individual cells underneath your headers and alter the formula in the ribbon, all you need to change is the location that the formula is pulling the number from and which column that the formula is finding the answer.

The formula for the sales column would be

$$= VLOOKUP(B3, Table1, 4, TRUE)$$

And the formula for the Pets column would be

$$= VLOOKUP(D3, Table1, 5, TRUE)$$

Random1	Random2	Random3	Cashier	Sales	Pet
0.289003	0.493576	0.016803	Lacy	76.81	Dog
0.364515	0.949465	0.575214	Tyler	28.11	Invertibre
0.904809	0.601099	0.895541	Shawn	82.98	Snake
0.426089	0.786577	0.278109	Chloe	31.97	Lizard
0.970172	0.391033	0.275682	Shawn	9.25	Lizard
0.030172	0.578074	0.79224	Lisa	16.96	Saltwater Fish
0.834707	0.148518	0.612407	Carol	53.8	Freshwater Fish
0.359783	0.864718	0.680122	Tyler	18.44	Freshwater Fish
0.575225	0.040708	0.180552	Merlin	46.95	Cat
0.177342	0.630623	0.900622	Donald	82.98	Exotic
0.037478	0.17313	0.444624	Lisa	53.8	Small Animal
0.072288	0.303035	0.562917	Lisa	9.25	Invertibre
0.513072	0.815949	0.268873	Merlin	18.44	Lizard
0.012632	0.29587	0.643942	Lisa	64.98	Freshwater Fish
0.471232	0.771847	0.642433	Chloe	31.97	Freshwater Fish
0.008652	0.115353	0.507678	Lisa	53.8	Invertibre
0.152774	0.220373	0.175495	Donald	64.98	Cat
0.25476	0.020152	0.464869	Lacy	46.95	Small Animal
0.811913	0.676638	0.662981	Carol	82.98	Freshwater Fish

Once you have altered the formulas you can click and highlight the altered cells release the left button on the mouse and then click the little square on the bottom right again and drag the outline on the cells all the way to the end of the columns. Your results should look similar to the table to the left. Remember, because we have the computer randomly selecting the numbers yours will not contain the exact same distribution of data the example does.

EXTRA NOTE: There are other controls that you can use in navigating your spreadsheet, by selecting one of the cells in the random data that we have created you can scroll up and down, left and right, by holding the control key and using the keyboard arrows. You can also highlight all the cells you want by holding the shift key while doing so.

Before we start making PivotTables though, we are going to go to the sales column and right click the letter for that column. Scroll down the little menu to format cells option and click on it. A window will pop up and will have a couple of different tabs but the one that comes up first is the number tab. There will be a scroll down list area and in the list will contain, General, Number, Currency, ect. You want to click on currency, feel free to choose any currency that you like that Excel provides. As stated at the beginning of this book it is encouraged that you fiddle with all the features and options that you can because that allows you to become more familiar with this process.

Quick Latin Lesson: Most everyone knows the word data, but does anyone actually know what it stands for? Data is actually the plural word for datum.

Data is most often used as a singular mass noun, though strangely enough it depends on what context you are using it for.

Chapter 3

Let's Pivot That Table

Creating Your First PivotTable

Now that we have 600 cells of random data, are you ready to set up your first PivotTable? Good!

We are going to highlight all the data first then go up to the menu bar and click on the insert tab. There's a button all the way over to the left that says PivotTable. there will be two option for you to create your PivotTable. The first is a blank PivotTable that allows you to custom make your table, the second is Excel will suggest different tables that will each focus of different things. Things like sales or the percentage of sales each cashier has. Reminder there is a limit as to what we can do with the data that we created.

In the picture shown here this is the message box that gives you the options of choosing between having your data appear either on the same worksheet that you are already on (with all of your data on it) or to place the PivotTable onto a new spread sheet. We are going to place this on a new spreadsheet so that we are not scrolling back and forth on the one spreadsheet and just need to click over from spreadsheet to spreadsheet.

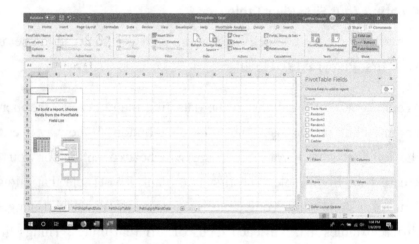

Originally your PivotTable does not look like a PivotTable, it looks more like the picture provided. The text box on the left says to create your report by selecting from the fields listed in the scroll list and drag them to the different quadrants. We covered fields earlier but to refresh the fields are the headers from your data and there are the quadrants of Filter, Columns, Rows, and Values. I've enlarged the righthand side of the picture, with the PivotTable Fields, so that you can see better what it looks like.

The first thing that we are going to is place the Cashiers field into the Rows and place Sales field into the Values, the result of this will give you the total sales each cashier has for the data that we created.

Row Labels ▾	Sum of Sales
Carol	$657.24
Chloe	$756.84
David	$1,462.98
Georgiana	$1,051.04
Lacey	$554.86
Lisa	$634.47
Merlin	$763.45
Mike	$1,072.35
Shawn	$974.64
Tyler	$849.11
Grand Total	$8,776.98

As you can see, it automatically labels your columns, and you can even change the label names if you wanted to just double left click to highlight the text and type in the title that you want.

From there we can also place into the Columns field Types of Pets and see what sales fall where. The chart below displays this. Wasn't that easy, it also keeps the total Sales so that you can make sure that all information correlates. To add onto the great things that your PivotTable can do is that you can change the currency values over to percentages by right clicking the table, it will pop up the same format cell message box from earlier, you can change the values over to percentages just as easily.

Sum of Sales	Column Labels										
Row Labels	Ball Python	Bearded Dragon	Budgie/Parakeet	Cat	Dog	Ferret	Fish	Hamster	Parrot	Saltwater	Grand Total
Carol		$239.89		$10.75	$138.09	$21.64	$43.58	$21.50	$181.79		$657.24
Chloe	$94.92	$101.50	$96.25	$47.87		$160.70		$154.10	$101.50		$756.84
David	$341.10	$176.54	$21.64	$154.05	$197.70	$79.44		$144.12	$241.76	$106.63	$1,462.98
Georgiana	$43.58	$157.80	$176.70	$57.80	$192.50	$122.25	$80.29	$96.25	$80.29	$43.58	$1,051.04
Lacey	$21.64	$43.58		$37.12	$96.84	$64.45			$117.41	$173.82	$554.86
Lisa					$101.93	$21.50	$176.54		$168.55	$165.95	$634.47
Merlin	$78.90	$43.58		$37.12	$101.50	$10.75		$89.65	$314.79	$87.16	$763.45
Mike		$57.80	$123.00	$91.04	$191.17	$101.50		$271.94	$139.65	$96.25	$1,072.35
Shawn	$155.01	$58.76		$10.75	$208.50	$238.20	$202.88			$100.54	$974.64
Tyler	$43.58		$57.80		$96.25		$240.19	$197.63	$133.37	$80.29	$849.11
Grand Total	$778.73	$879.45	$549.63	$672.53	$1,088.66	$755.98	$743.48	$975.19	$1,479.11	$854.22	$8,776.98

Now, remember how at the beginning we wanted to see how the cashiers were doing in their average sales, or even see who were your top cashiers? By clicking the dropdown box for the Row Labels, you can choose who you want to include and who you want to exclude. The picture to the right, you can see that the dropdown menu allows you to sort the list A to Z, Z to A and even customize how you want it sorted.

Below in the list box you can choose who you want to keep on your chart or who you want to remove from the list. You can also go into the part labeled Value Filters and you can pick your Top 10 Salespeople, or you can go into more sort options and order your salespeople from highest sales to the lowest. You didn't even need to do any sort of math to figure out who they were! The PivotTable did it for you.

Different Charts

Before we completely move on to making charts we are going to go over the types of charts that Excel provides because we are definitely not going to cover all of them and we are also going to be going over the "anatomy" of a chart so that you will know what has been adjusted in the charts that are featured in this text. As it was said earlier, Excel offers a number of different charts but not all the charts display the same thing, while one might display how much you made in sales last month versus this month. While another might show when your sales drop during the week and you can figure out different ways to boost it.

To add onto the confusion there are multiple types of data that you can chart, examples are characteristics, numbers, locations, times/dates. Even then some of your data can relate to another piece of data, so then you would have to set up a hierarchy system to see which data either has more value or occurs first. Even that depends on what type of data you are dealing with or what you deem as more valuable. You surprisingly can chart all the information in this book if you wanted to.

Bar charts have three different versions:

Bar Chart	Represents data in a horizontal fashion and in various sizes. Best if used when you have long titles for categories or wish to display information in the bars.
Column Chart	Represents data in a vertical fashion and in various sizes. Best for using if you have similar categories in your data that you want separated.
Stacked Bar Chart	Similar to the two before it only in this case the similar categories count for a whole and so they are stacked upon each other.
Line Chart	Displays data as a marker and then connects those markers with a line. Can be used to display a variety of data, mostly over time.
Pie (Donut)	A circular graph that is meant to represent a numerical whole and the slices represent the numerical parts of data that create the whole. A donut is the same only it has a hole cut out of it.

Area	Looks like a map for elevations only it displays your data in measurable way.
X & Y (Scatter Plot)	Similar to the line chart, it displays your data through coordinates set by the values on the X and Y axis, without having to connect the data.
Map	In the newer versions of Excel, if you have locational data in your table this allows you reference an actual map. From there you can have the map display a number of different things, like sales or which location has the highest return customers,
Box and Whisker (Stock)	Also known as a box plot or stock graph, this type of chart allows you to show not only the solid numbers from your data but the possible highs and lows of those numbers as well.
Surface	This type of chart plots your data like it is the ground in an older video game, it is rendered in a three-dimensional way but if you alter the angle you look at your character it shows that there is nothing below the surface.
Radar	This chart allows you to see multiple characteristics of data at the same time, most recently it has been used to display enneagram results.
Tree Map	Similar to the funnel chart the tree map, instead of cutting out the excluded data, boxes all the into different sections, in a hierarchical like fashion.

Sunburst	Also, for hierarchical data, this is set in multiple rings with the top of the chain being in the center of the rings. Though if it only has one type of data it looks like a sad Donut chart
Histogram	These charts are kind of a cross between bar and line charts but are actually showing the range of where the data falls. The best example of this is if you are hitting a baseball or golf balls, say you hit 100 balls and that someone (not a machine) was giving the balls to you at different speeds, where those balls land in the field and the rate that they are hit is what makes a histogram.
Waterfall	These types of charts are unique in the fact that they allow you to see what happens when you add in positive and negative factors to your chart.
Funnel	Funnel charts are exactly as they sound, they start with a broad spectrum of data and then narrow it down to what you what you specifically want to include.
Combo	Amazingly Excel offers this special feature, it combines two charts together which allows you to display more than one concept at a time.

Chart Anatomy

You now know about the different types of charts that Excel offers and what types of data they can display. The next thing to learn is the anatomy of a chart, this will assist you when you are changing your charts up later because some of the Excel program does list all the different areas on the chart when you right click it. But, if you do not know what part of the chart that it is, how is that supposed to help you?

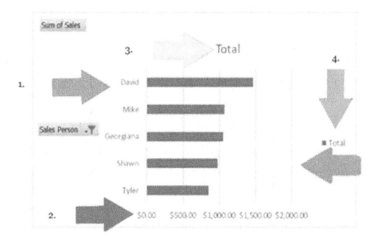

The picture provided for you is to assist you in learning the anatomy of a chart. The arrows point at different parts and are colored so that you can see them a little easier.

Starting at the top and moving clockwise we begin with the yellow arrow pointing to the title. Then next is the green that is pointing to the legend, followed by the blue which is pointing towards where the data sits on the chart. The Red arrow is pointing to X axis which is where one of your parts of measurement can go or one of your categories. The orange arrow is pointing to the Y axis that allows you to also place a measurement or a category.

Those are the main parts of the table, but they are not the only parts that are customizable. Going back to the blue arrow that points to your charting area, there are a variety of different thing that you can do to customize how you want it viewed. You can change all the colors of the bars, make them bigger or smaller (relative to the picture, it will not alter your data), change the space between them and even place labels in the bars. You can also remove the graph lines if you wanted to and the Pivot chart buttons. You can add on labels for the X and Y axis. There is a whole assortment that you can do and you will be encouraged to mettle with it all later on.

Right now however, we are going to be moving on to creating your first graph, it's actually going to come out just like the one above (sorry for ruining the surprise), and you will be able to alter it in any way you please.

Altering the PivotTable

Now, lets get the Top 5, because we only have 10 cashiers in our list, and we are going to change it into a bar chart so that it is nicely displayed. First, we are going to remove pet type from the columns field so we just have the cashiers and sum of sales on a table. Great, now we are going to narrow our ten cashiers down to our Top 5.

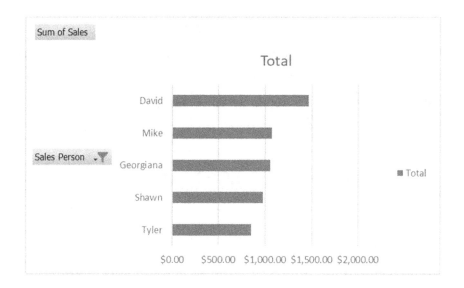

First, we are going to highlight the table and then hit the insert tab and click the little down arrow next to the bar chart icon. Here we just want the basic bar chart to begin with, later on you can work with the 3D ones, once you get this part down.

The graph displayed is what you should originally pop out. As explained in the last section from here we can customize the chart anyway we want. We can change the colors of the bars, remove the dropdown boxes and change the title of the chart. We can change where the totals are displayed and even have it say what the exact totals are.

The picture that is below is the one that has been edited and altered by myself, I deleted the money increments at the bottom of the chart along with the lines. I hid the fields buttons and added the cashier's totals onto the end of their bars. You can alter all of this by right clicking directly on the item that you want to select and changing them in the menus that appear. I also changed the colors of the bars from blue to various colors and the title from Total to Top 5 Cashiers. The title portion you can change by double clicking, so that the title is highlighted and typing in a title of your choice. You can even move it around to where you want it to be placed.

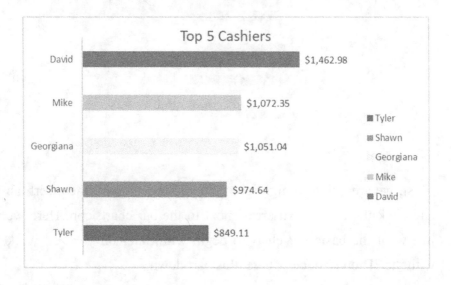

Voila, you have now created your first chart from your PivotTable. You are now on your way to making an interactive dashboard. Next up, we are going to create a pie chart to show which type of pet sells best in the store. We are also going to show you how to add an extra column into your data and how to have that column be added onto your PivotTable's fields.

Chapter 4

What It All Breaks Down To

Who wants some pie?

First what we are going to do is go back to our data to copy and paste our original pivot chart to a new sheet, this will allow you to have plenty of room and you will not have to be scrolling around to get back and forth. To easily copy your pivot chart go down to where your tab is for your sheet, hold down the left mouse button and drag the sheet to the right a bit, while holding your mouse button down hit the control key, the little page icon should go from having nothing on it to have a little plus (+) sign. Ta-da, you have now created a new sheet with a copy of your PivotTable, and we didn't even need to go back to our original data to create the new PivotTable.

Row Labels ⌄↑	Sum of Sales
Ball Python	$778.73
Bearded Dragon	$879.45
Budgie/Parakeet	$549.63
Cat	$672.53
Dog	$1,088.66
Ferret	$836.27
Fish	$663.19
Hamster	$975.19
Parrot	$1,479.11
Saltwater	$854.22
Grand Total	$8,776.98

For creating this pie chart, we are going to place the type of pet into the rows and the value is going to be the sum of the sales. The chart that you come up with should be something like this first chart:

Row Labels	⬇	Sum of Sales
Parrot		$1,479.11
Dog		$1,088.66
Hamster		$975.19
Bearded Dragon		$879.45
Saltwater		$854.22
Ferret		$836.27
Ball Python		$778.73
Cat		$672.53
Fish		$663.19
Budgie/Parakeet		$549.63
Grand Total		**$8,776.98**

However, this chart is only in alphabetical order and it isn't quite what I want. What I really want, is to be able to see the top sellers (the types of animals) that the shop caters to. So, we are going to go to the top of the table and left click on the row label dropdown menu, after the first sorting options, click the option that allows for different sorting features. Once you have clicked on it a little window should pop up and it will give you the option buttons of ascending and descending along with dropdown menus that ask if you want it by the pet or by the sum of sales. You want the descending option with the sum of sales.

Your result should be something similar to this second list, it should have all types of pets listed in descending order from highest sales to lowest.

Now if I wanted to I could narrow this list down further like I did before and have it show me just the top five sellers on my list but we are going to create a variety on this pie chart so that it allows you to play with it a bit more in customizing it to what you would like. Like it was said before the more you work with this program's option for your charts the more familiar you become with it and the more proficient you become at it.

Trucking on, highlight the table and once again click the insert tab and click the little down arrow next to the pie chart. Again, you will see several different options on pie charts aside from 2D and 3D, there will also be the option for the donut chart. In this example we are just going to do a simple pie chart.

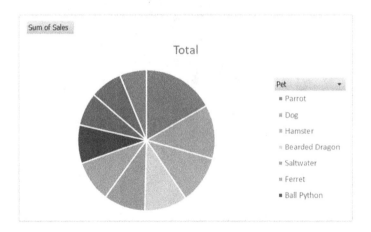

This image below is the pie chart that came out, is not very attractive in its colors and does not really expand upon what it is that we are looking at. To add to the confusion some of the sale totals are so close you cannot tell what type of pet the is the better consumer.

So, lets fix it up.

What I am going to do is alter the title from Total to Consumer Pet Sales. I'm also going to make sure that the field buttons are invisible, we do not really need them. Next is to change the colors and have a label that will clearly display the sales for each of the pets is going to be listed inside the pieces.

Just as a heads up, in the newer version of Excel you have to double click the pieces of the pie chart twice in order to properly select the piece you want. If you do not then most likely what will happen is your whole chart will turn one color.

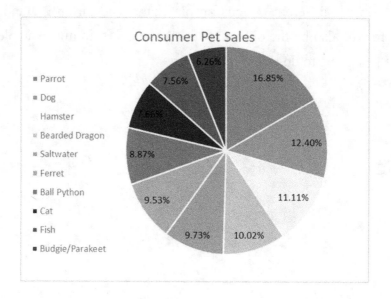

Want to know how to switch this from just being about sales to what percentage each pet
has contributed to sales?

Going back to our PivotTable Fields menu we have to change the values area from where it is set on sum and change it over to percentage, we do this by clicking on the Sum of Sales dropdown menu button and select the Value Field settings. From there a window will pop up and the part that you are looking for is the second tab that is offered. The tab should say Show Value As, once on that tab you can select the dropdown menu and ask the computer to show you the percent of the total.

Let's add some more

There is one type of data missing from our chart from earlier that we cannot really do without while keeping a Pet supply store. That type of data is the measurement of time, this addition of data will allow us to make another set of charts because we added another facet to the data.

Week Ending
5/4/2019
5/11/2019
5/18/2019
5/25/2019
6/1/2019

For us to do this we are going to go back to our original set of data and after the Pet column add a week ending Column.

What we are going to do with this column is put the Saturdays in May of 2019 into this column, that dates that you need are 5/4/19, 5/11/19, 5/18/19, 5/25/19 and 6/1/19, going down the column you will need to place one date in and then copy the data for 30 rows using the drag and drop method. This will allow us to have five weeks' worth of data. I know that this isn't realistic, but we are starting off easy.

Now that we have that five weeks' worth of data, we can now create a new PivotTable. This time head back to the sheet that you have your pie chart on and copy that sheet as we did before. Now you can remove the extra pie table that you have by cutting it out or selecting it and hitting the backspace button, either way you just need to make it go away.

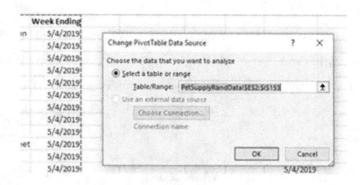

The easiest way to do this is to click on one of the cells in the table that is still on your spread sheet. Then go up to the top of the Excel window and select the tab that says PivotTable Analyze, once you have switched over to that table you should see a button that say Change Data Source. Once you click on it you should get a window that looks familiar. It's similar to the window that popped up when we originally made our PivotTable. This action will also bring you back to your source data page (where the computer is getting all its data references), from there you can add on that last row that we just created into the ribbon that has the highlighted text or you can click on the little up arrow and it will allow you to manually select the range that you want once again. When you are all done you can click the OK button and Excel will automatically add that field to your PivotTable Fields menu.

Let's Line it Up

Onward to the next basic chart, the Line chart. Most of the time I associate these with heart monitors, because it shows the contraction of your four heat chambers over a period of time. They are also used in sales and to show growth rates of plants, urban area population and children. There are many different uses for a line chart, we are just going to be showing the growth of sales over time.

Time to copy our PivotTable again and remove the pie chart and bring up the Pivot Table menu. This time we going to keep our Sum of Sales in the value quadrant of the PivotTable Field menu but we need to go back into its Field Value Settings and change the display of the data from the percentage that we had it on previously for the pie chart, under the tab labeled show values as you just want to set the dropdown menu back to the no calculation setting.

After completing that you place the Week ending data in the Rows quadrant and the pets into the Columns quadrant. This will allow you to see all the pets and their sales over the past five weeks. Now you may have some pound signs in some of the cells on your table, this is okay because we can fix it, just right click the table and a short menu will appear, select the PivotTable Format option, new window will appear afterwards. In the window there should be several different tabs but the one we want should be the one that appears first. Visually scrolling down the window there should be two check boxes that allow you to type in what you want if there is no data available or if an error has occurred in the calculations, check both and place a " " in the space. This will allow the box to stay blank and you will not have to worry about the pound signs showing up again.

Note: For all those who do not know a pound sign is #. It is not a hashtag.

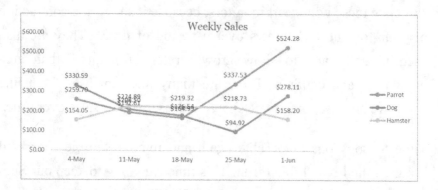

Before we turn this into a line chart narrow this down to your top three. This will allow you to have fewer lines on your chart, you will be able to see what is going where and it will allow you to be able to click on the different aspects that you wish to change on the lines.

What you can see from the table that came out for me is that some of the numbers are on top of each other but fortunately the colors that the computer used have enough contrast that you can see clearly where they lead to. The legend is a little far off, we should fix the title, and we can adjust where the numbers for the markers fall.

Addressing the parts that we need to tweak, starting with the legend there is a little plus sign next to the top right corner of your chart. Once you click on it, it shows all of the chart's "elements". Remember how we went over a chart's anatomy, all those terms and parts that were shown before? This is where those come into play, all those terms are now in a neat little list.

Moving on, what you want is to go to where the legend check box is and click off on it. When you click on that it makes the legend disappear, don't worry we are going to do something a little different. Still on the chart elements go up a little bit and select the Data Table options. What this does is it places all your data points into a grid below your dates and it adds a legend. If you double click on the table a little side menu pops up called the Format Chart Area; there is a little box option underneath the title. By selecting that box icon it will open up the area that will give you the options of changing the grid's height and length.

Next is going to be moving the numbers so that you can see them clearer, one of the best things is that Excel will automatically place a thin line connecting the number that you have moved to its marker. Another thing is that once you click on one of the numbers that is associated with one of your plot lines, Excel selects the series of them. This allows you to easily tell which numbers go to which line on your line graph, adding on to this you can also change the color of the numbers.

From the picture above you can see that I have actually followed through with the instructions that we just went through.

Chapter 5

On the Dashboard

Congratulations. You have made it all the way here and this is where you learn to place all of your charts onto a Dashboard with interactive Slicers. Now we defined slicers at the beginning of the book as interactive buttons that allow you to interact with the data displayed on the dashboard; often times it is referred to being able to slice and dice data.

Now this is where we walk you through making your own Dashboard. First create a new spread sheet and make Row 1 of that spread sheet a bit wider so that you can place (pet store's name) Sales Review. Once you stretch that out you can highlight the cells across the top of that spread sheet, and right click to allow you to pick and choose your font and if you like, different colors for the font and/or the cell color.

From there we can go to each of our spread sheets that have our charts, to select and drag, or cut and paste all 3 of our charts onto the dashboard. The cheat that I use to make the charts look like they are evenly spaced is to use the grid lines from the spread sheet. Later on, I'll tell you how to make the lines go away but for now we want them there.

Spark Lines

As a side note, one of the things that Excel offers is something called a spark line and this little guy is pretty cool. A Spark line allows you to place a line graph inside of a cell. Though most of the time what you want is to have access to a larger more detailed data reference, we can create another line chart just to do an example. What we are going to do now is go to our sheet with the PivotTable that contains the line chart that we created earlier. Once there we go to the Insert tab, then mostly to the right and after the 3D Map option should be the category marked Sparklines. Within that category are three options Lines, Column and Win/Loss; the one that we want is the Line one. Now I know it doesn't look like much and with the data that we have we are just repeating creating a line chart but like I stated earlier I would rather you know how to do this or be over informed of the information rather than need to create one and not know how to do it.

So, creating a Sparkline is fairly simple, we already have our table of data that is needed to create it, all we need to do now is highlight the data. But before doing that let's remove the filter for the top three and get all of our pets back on the board. Now all we want just the Grand Total of the weeks listed (just not the Grand Grand Total) once those numbers are highlighted you can go and click the line option in the Sparklines. What should happen is that you should get a little pop up window stating that you highlighted the cells that your Grand Total is in and it will be asking you where you want to place your Sparkline.

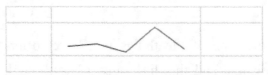

3 Promise I tried to clean this up and make it look
nice. It didn't work but you now know what a
Sparkline looks like.

You can feel free to place it on the sheet that you are on or you can place it on the sheet with your Dashboard. Once you okay it, there should be a nice little line within the cell you selected. Isn't it cute? Kidding.

If you just placed the Sparkline on the sheet that we were working on you can just cut and paste the line right onto your Dashboard and in the cell above it type in Totals Trending. So that people can now see the totals trending for the sales of that store.

Slicers

Last, but not least, the whole reason for this is Slicers. Slicers allow your whole Dashboard to be interactive. They can allow anyone to look at different data points and different factors.

Before creating these though I want you to go back through your sheets and for the Pie chart and Bar chart add on the weekly data before we go any further. This is so that when we create our slicers they interact with all the charts at the same time. Click back over to your Dashboard and refresh too. You can do this by right clicking on the chart and at the top of the menu should be an option to refresh the chart.

After doing this you can bring up the PivotTable Field menu from your Line chart. When it appears go to the scrolling list area where all of your Fields are listed and right click on the Pet field. A menu should appear from it and listed towards the bottom will be the option of "Add a Slicer". Click that and you should have a little box with Pet listed at the top with all your "pet" options listed in that little box. You can now place that little box where-ever you please on your Dashboard, and when you click on it, it should make your Top 5 Cashiers chart change a bit. It will show what their sales for that particular animal was.

In addition, if we go and right click on the Pie chart and bring up its PivotChart Fields you can right click on the week ending Field and create a new Slicer for that. That will allow you to see the different weeks and which pet sold better during the week that you selected.

Remember I told you that I would show you how to get rid of those pesky grid lines? There are two different ways that we can make them go away, first you can go to the View tab at the top of your screen and in there, there's a check box for the grid lines, uncheck the box and all the grid lines go away. The second is you can go to the box located underneath where we placed our title for the dashboard and select all the cells outwards until you have covered the area your Dashboard is in. The next part you can do from the Home tab and you can color in your cells with any color you please. You want it red, make it red, teal for your favorite college colors, no problem. It is completely up to you, though most of the time you will probably want it white if you are doing this for work.

For a grand finale I didn't want anyone to thing that their Dashboard looked bad and I kept mine rough with you guys in mind. It's a little rough looking but everything is lined up and both the Slicers are placed next to the charts that they correspond to.

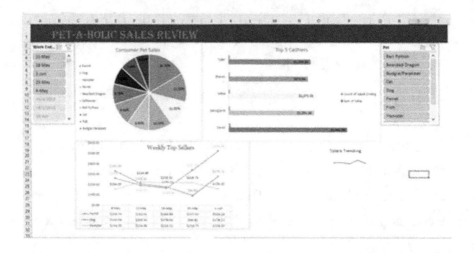

Practice, Practice, Practice

Remember to keep practicing with all the parts of making PivotTables and Dashboards. It is always encouraged to keep working at something until you get it. You were even given a way to practice without having to search the internet for hours looking for the perfect data base. Go ahead and create a table with several different locations and a completely different concept. You can add a map onto your Dashboard and have that be interactive, make Sparkline Bar charts and anything you want in 3D.

Chapter 6

Always Have Options

A dded into this chapter are several different things that will aid you in creating your PivotTables and Dashboards. There are things like ad-ons from programmers, who specifically created the ad-ons to help people in what they want to create with their PivotTable. Things like YouTube videos that you can reference if you didn't understand the concept or felt that I did not cover some thing enough. Also, included in this chapter is some references for randomizing your data or helping you with selecting names, numbers or places (I tend to use alliteration when I write in names/places). And even a link to the list of functions that Excel contains, now all at your fingertips.

Note: None of these websites/references endorsed this book and were used a reference only, ninety eight percent of the pictures in this book were provided by the author and the other two percent were cited in the picture's comments.

Always Check your Add-ons

This sounds like a weird concept, but I promise it isn't. There are people out there who create their own add-ons and then market them to basic users. The add-ons can be for anything, like taking a form that you scanned and having all the information from that form be added right into your Excel sheet, or having an ad-on that has ready made templates for you to use. Things like this make it this make it easier for the beginners, and the inept to be able to create whatever they please. Note: some of these you will either have ads or you will need to pay for them.

Pivot Pal was in one of the YouTube videos that will be in the reference notes

https://www.excelcampus.com/pivotpal/

These two were added in after a search and a quick review:

https://www.contextures.com/xlPivotPremAddIn.html

https://www.add-ins.com/pivot-table-assistant.htm

Easy Cheats

So easy cheats aren't so easy. This is really just a list of functions that you can use while in Excel, say like you wanted to reference some data or have the equations of something be rounded down instead of up. That's what you would use these functions for. Also listed is a bunch of "Random" sites, that allow you to pick random data for you to use, not the database kind but the kind that helps you put the table that makes your random database together.

This first link is from the official Office website. It contains all the functions in alphabetical order with the added information of what it is best suited for and what it does:

https://support.office.com/en-gb/article/excel-functions-alphabetical-b3944572-255d-4efb-bb96-c6d90033e188

There are even keyboard shortcuts for you to make your way through Excel even easier and to cut down on you having to constantly switch between the mouse and the keyboard:

https://www.howtogeek.com/361582/all-the-best-microsoft-excel-keyboard-shortcuts/

The next links are to assist you in compiling your base data for you to create your table. The first gives you an assortment of options but can be limited in certain aspects:

https://www.random.org/lists/

This one is to public data but it is a website you have to pay for:

https://login.publicdata.com/

Just as a reminder there are public records that you can access for the state, it may be a few years old but should still be a good reference, most of the information though deals with police investigation and the such.

This next one website has a list of public data bases that you can look at and use. I did not look through them all so you may need to pay for some if you have a mind to use that particular data:

https://www.columnfivemedia.com/100-best-free-data-sources-infographic

Explaining It Better

Not everyone learns the same, for me it's the see one, do one, teach one, method that works best for me. This concept is usually pretty self-explanatory but to clarify for those who don't quite get the concept the method is:

See one- See how something is done once, allowing you to understand the concept that you are being taught.

Do one- You have seen how something is done, now it's time to do it on your own, to master this concept.

Teach one- Now that you have the concept down, try teaching it to someone else, this allows you to know that you know how to do the task, but it also allows you to see if you know how to correctly teach it and if the other person is having a problem you can look at it and either adjust how to teach it or you didn't fully understand as much as you thought.

Though sometimes its just a communication error, and you need it to be taught to you a different way. The reference video for pivot tables that I am providing off of the YouTube website is from a Mynda Treacy. She previously received an award from Microsoft as an MVP for teaching over twenty-five thousand students online about the Excel program and that was back in 2014. Today, she has taught over seventy-five thousand students and has her own web teaching course and webinars if you wish to attend.

https://www.youtube.com/watch?v=K74_FNnlIF8&t=2143s

The randomizing data process was utilized by Tiger Spreadsheet Solutions via YouTube:

https://www.youtube.com/watch?v=mbv9rnwrRNg

In addition to the website above, I also located a website that offers different focuses as to what you want your dashboard to be about. This particular website offers to have different focuses such as, social media and customer success:

https://chartio.com/learn/dashboards-and-charts/

References

Last but not least are references that were used in compiling the data for this book. Most of the information was gleaned through the YouTube videos above but the resources also include:

General information on PivotTables:
https://en.wikipedia.org/wiki/Pivot_table

Information on William Playfair:
https://en.wikipedia.org/wiki/William_Playfair

Definitions were all pulled off the Merriam-Webster dictionary website:
https://www.merriam-webster.com/

Another YouTube video that was utilized in making this book was Excel Campus by Jon, this person also created the Pivot Pal and will also show you how his add-on works and the best ways to use it:
https://www.youtube.com/watch?v=FyggutiBKvU

Again, some of the websites listed in the easy cheats and explaining it better were utilized in the making of this book as well.

Always remember to practice, even when you get everything down pat, a skill that is not used, becomes dull and after a while.

Conclusion

Congratulations on making your way all the way to the conclusion of this book. It is not often enough that people truly read their way all the way through a book now a days and you should be proud of that. As always, I hope that the information that you gained from my book will assist you and that you benefit from it.

Before leaving you guys to make your way in creating your own PivotTables and interactive Dashboards, I wanted to thank you again for choosing this book in helping. Wanting to teach those that are willing to learn is such a huge reason why this book happened. I hope you enjoyed it and will recommend it to others.

Once again, because I am pretty sure that I said it in the beginning of this book, I wish that everyone is happy and healthy. And that everyone continues to be so in this crazy and hectic world that we live in.

I really do enjoy teaching you guys, about anything that you will allow me to teach you. I believe that if we all kept learning and teaching, we will better understand the world around us, and this will aid in our communication with each other.

Finally, before you leave the book, remember that it would be greatly appreciated for you to go back to Amazon and give us a review. Remember that any type of constructive feedback is good feedback and I want to improve along with you guys that are learning.

Thank you and good luck!